CW01658654

Lizzy, Darcy and Jane

A play

Joanna Norland

Samuel French — London
www.samuelfrench-london.co.uk

ISBN 978 0 573 11233 1

Please see page iv for further copyright information

LIZZY, DARCY AND JANE

Lizzy, Darcy and Jane was developed and was first produced by JaMaM Productions with funding from Arts Council England under the working title *Jane Austen Makes a Match*, 16 September - 4 November 2006, with the following cast:

Jane	Clare Cameron
Elizabeth	Kerry Steed
Mr Bingley/ Harris/ Mr Collins	James Kleinmann
Mr Darcy/ Tom	Simon Balcan
Mrs Austen/ Cassandra	Nicola Borthwick
Madame Lefroy/ Lady Catherine/ Alethea	Suzanne Tooney

Directed and produced by Carol Hall
Costumes: Sue Sherwin
Choreographers: Ellis and Christine Rogers
Dramaturge: Deirdre Strath Clyde
Consulting Historian: John White

It was also produced by C Company at the Tabard Theatre, London, 8 January - 2 February 2008, with the following cast:

Jane	Aileen Gonsalves
Elizabeth	Susan Bracken
Mr Bingley/ Harris/ Mr Collins	Zak Rowlands
Mr Darcy/ Tom	Alex Trippier
Mrs Austen/ Alethea	Sheridan Macdonald
Madame Lefroy/ Lady Catherine/ Cassandra	Jo Nuttall

Directed by Marie McCarthy
Set Design: Mark Simmonds
Costume Design: Libby Lee
Movement Director: Helen Heaslip
Lighting: Tom Nickson
Sound: Daniel Tomlinson

(See also page ii)

CHARACTERS

Jane Austen, 20 in Act I and 26 in Act II
Mr Bingley, 25
Mr Darcy, 27 in Act I, 34 and then 27 in Act II
Elizabeth Bennet, 20 in Act I, 26 and then 20 in Act II
Harris Bigg-Wither, 15 in Act I and 21 in Act II
Tom Lefroy, 20
Mrs Austen, 40
Madame Lefroy, Tom's aunt, 50
Mr Collins, 25
Lady Catherine de Bourgh, Mr Darcy's aunt, 50
Alethea Bigg-Wither, Harris's sister, 35
Cassandra Austen, Jane's sister, 28

Multiple roles may be played by certain actors to highlight the connections between Jane Austen's life and fiction. For example, the following roles may be played by a single actor:

Mr Darcy and **Tom Lefroy**
Mr Bingley, **Harris** and **Mr Collins**
Madame Lefroy, **Lady Catherine** and **Alethea**
Mrs Austen and **Cassandra**

The staging in the script uses the above multiple role-playing. Other role allocations are possible, or the roles may be assigned to one actor each, with adjustments to the stage directions.

SYNOPSIS OF SCENES

ACT I

Scene 1 January 1796. Evening. The ballroom in the home of the Bigg-Withers
Scene 2 The following morning. The parlour in the Austens' home

ACT II

December 1802. Evening. The drawing room in the home of the Bigg-Withers

Notes on Staging

Characters in this play include figures from Jane Austen's circle (the real characters) and from *Pride and Prejudice* (the fictional characters). As indicated in the cast list, some of the actors may assume one or more "real" and "fictional" roles, though the actors playing Jane and Elizabeth, respectively, should not play any other roles. The fictional characters (Mr Darcy, Mr Bingley, Elizabeth, Mr Collins and Lady Catherine) can see and hear the real characters, but the real characters (other than Jane and, at the end of Act II, Cassandra) cannot see or hear the fictional characters. Only Jane interacts with both the real and fictional characters.

If actors assume multiple roles, they will often shift between roles while on stage. If an actor playing one role (e.g. Mr Darcy) shifts to a different role (e.g. Tom Lefroy) while on stage, the entrance of the second character is not indicated in the stage directions. If each role is assigned to a different actor (i.e. with a cast of twelve), additional entrances and/or exits will be required.

About Jane Austen

Jane Austen was born at Steventon Parsonage in Hampshire on December 16, 1775, to the Reverend George Austen, a clergyman of modest means, and his wife, Cassandra, members of the lesser gentry. The second youngest child in a family of two daughters and six sons, Jane Austen began writing in her youth. At the age of 20, she began *First Impressions*, an early version of *Pride and Prejudice*. In 1801, her parents left Steventon Parsonage for Bath with their two unmarried daughters, Jane, and her beloved older sister, named Cassandra after their mother. The ensuing years were an unsettled time for them all. The family changed quarters repeatedly, and it is believed that for a time, Jane Austen virtually ceased writing.

In 1809, Jane's brother Edward, who had come into wealth, provided a home for his now-widowed mother and two unmarried sisters in Chawton, Hampshire. Jane Austen lived there until her death in 1817, publishing *Sense and Sensibility* in 1811, *Pride and Prejudice* in 1813, *Mansfield Park* in 1814, *Emma* in 1815, and *Persuasion* and *Northanger Abbey* posthumously, in 1818. *Lizzy, Darcy and Jane* draws on key events in Jane Austen's life, including her romance with Tom Lefroy in 1796 and Harris Bigg-Wither's proposal in 1802. As no manuscripts of *First Impressions* or *Pride and Prejudice* have survived, we know almost nothing about how the novel developed and changed between its inception and publication. This aspect of the play is my invention.

J.N.

Acknowledgements

I am grateful to Arts Council England, South East, for generously supporting the research and development of this play, to various members of the Jane Austen Society (UK) for assisting me with my research, to Peter Thompson and the Player Playwrights theatre group in London, England for enabling me to workshop an early draft of this script, and to my dramaturge, Deirdre Strath Clyde, my mentor, Peter Vincent, and my colleague, Lara Muth, for their invaluable criticism, advice, and encouragement. I am indebted to Ellis Rogers, Christine Rogers, and John White for their guidance on Regency dance and history, as well as to the many actors who workshopped this script, and to JaMaM Productions and C Company for producing it. Finally, I would like to thank my mother, Roslyn Molinoff, for introducing me to *Pride and Prejudice*, my father, Joseph Norland, for reassuring me, during my long dormant spell, that I would find my way back to playwriting, my son, Alistair Duncan McLeod, for napping while I finished the script, and my husband, Alistair Scott McLeod, for loving Elizabeth Bennet — and me.

J.N.

ACT I

Scene 1

The ballroom at the home of the Bigg-Withers, a wealthy landed family. Evening, January 1796

As the play begins, dance music plays in the background. The music fades gradually. There is a game table, UL, *with three chairs. Depending on space available, the stage may also be set* UR *for Scene 2 (currently in darkness), with a writing desk equipped with pens, paper and an inkwell (far right) and three chairs. By the middle chair, there is a pile of garments for mending and a workbasket. When Scene 2 begins, actors may shift the Scene 2 furniture to a more central position. If space is not permitting, actors can remove the furniture and props from Scene 1 when they exit at the end of Scene 1 and bring on the furniture and props for Scene 2*

The actors playing Madame Lefroy, Mr Bingley/Harris/Mr Collins and Mr Darcy/Tom sit at the game table. Each holds a hand of cards

Jane enters

Jane Impossible man. Intolerable man. I have walked by the game table three times tonight, and not once did Mr Lefroy look up from his cards. If I do not please him, why did he invite me to dance twice at the Heartleys' ball last week? And if I do please him, why does he now insist on playing cards? I wish that men at balls behaved more like men in novels. My Mr Bingley always chooses dancing over cards. Is that not so, Mr Bingley? (*Louder*) I said, is that not so, Mr Bingley?

Mr Bingley rises from the game table and approaches Jane

Mr Bingley Most definitely. Particularly with so many lovely ladies assembled.

Jane Thank you, Mr Bingley. You always say the most enchanting things.

Mr Bingley Miss Jane Austen is too kind.

Jane Your charm should not surprise me. The moment I penned your name, I decided that you should be the most charming man in the world. And to settle the matter, I gave you an income of five thousand pounds a year.

Mr Bingley Is that my income? I can never recall the exact figure.

Jane It is in your nature to be affable, not precise.

Mr Bingley It is in my nature to dance. I have been ever so impatient for a ball.

Jane Shame on me! I promised you a ball to welcome you to your new neighbourhood!

Mr Bingley On page seventeen, you mentioned that there was soon to be a gathering at the Assembly Rooms. Only then —

Jane I set my novel aside for days. My excuse was that the Bigg-Withers had petitioned me to write a winter theatrical. But even that remains unfinished. Instead, I squandered my time flirting with my Irish friend. I am glad that Mr Lefroy leaves for Lincoln's Inn next week — (*mimicking Tom*) "to devote himself to the mysteries of the law."

Mr Bingley He will regret the wasted opportunity to dance when he is forced to burrow in the library.

Jane (*inspired*) I will be avenged yet. That is what novels are for. I will give you a conceited, arrogant friend who always refuses to dance. A failing for which he will be universally derided.

Mr Darcy rises from the game table and approaches Jane and Mr Bingley

You are far too serious to dance, are you not ... Mr ... Mr Darcy?

Mr Darcy Dancing does not suit all tastes or moods.

Jane Mr Darcy has never cared for dancing. (*To Mr Bingley*) Even when you first met ... at Cambridge.

Mr Bingley In my first year. Michaelmas term.

Mr Darcy It was I who first acquainted Bingley with the alarming intelligence that our college possessed a library.

Mr Bingley If it wasn't for Darcy, I should never have known that our college even had a library, let alone that I was meant to be a patron. But he is a capital fellow, I assure you.

Jane I do not think that all of Mr Darcy's acquaintances would agree.

Mr Darcy I consider their censure a relief, given the quality of their judgment on other matters.

Mr Bingley Do not pay Darcy any mind. This is always his manner upon a first meeting.

Jane His manners could not please me more. They accentuate your charm. Jane Bennet will notice the contrast between you when she meets you both at the ball.

Mr Bingley Is it certain that the eldest Miss Bennet will attend?

Mr Darcy I cannot imagine that she has any competing engagements.

Jane Of course my pretty heroine will be there. Accompanied by her three sisters, Mary, Kitty, and Lydia.

Mr Bingley The entire neighbourhood talks of her beauty.

Mr Darcy The entire neighbourhood cannot supply many alternative subjects of conversation.

Jane When you are introduced to Miss Jane Bennet, Mr Bingley, you will not disagree with the report that she is uncommonly handsome. (*She adopts the role of Jane Bennet and curtsies*)

Mr Bingley Good-evening, Miss Bennet.

Jane Good-evening, Mr Bingley.

Mr Bingley (*to Mr Darcy*) Handsome? Why she is the most beautiful creature I ever beheld. (*He holds out his hand to Jane in introduction*) Miss Bennet, I am delighted to form your acquaintance.

Music begins. Mr Bingley and Jane begin to dance

Jane We are honoured that you attend our assembly this evening, sir.

Mr Bingley I am ever so fond of dancing.

Jane (*as herself*) To be fond of dancing is a certain step towards falling in love.

Mr Bingley What an enchanting evening, Miss Bennet! (*Aside to Mr Darcy*) And what an enchanting lady.

Jane (*resuming the role of Jane Bennet*) I hope you will be happy in Hampshire, sir.

Mr Bingley Are balls in Hampshire always this lively?

Mr Darcy And are they always this long, and attended by such tiresome company?

Music ends abruptly

Jane (*as herself, breaking away from Mr Bingley, who joins Mr Darcy*) Tiresome ... Does Mr Lefroy also thinks us tiresome?

Mr Bingley Come, Darcy, I must have you dance. I hate to see you standing about by yourself in this stupid manner. You had much better dance.

Mr Darcy I certainly shall not. At such an assembly as this it would be insupportable.

Mr Bingley You jest!

Mr Darcy There is not a woman in the room whom it would not be a punishment to me to stand up with.

Elizabeth enters

Jane I suppose that, like Mr Darcy, Mr Lefroy prefers the fine ladies of London. Of course he does. (*She takes out a handkerchief and begins to cry*) And to make matters worse, young Harris Bigg-Wither ambushed me at the punch bowl and insisted that I save him a dance. If only my sister, Cassandra, were here. Cassandra would know how to advise me.

Elizabeth I hope that she would upbraid you sharply first. Fancy making yourself wretched on account of a young bachelor who plants himself at the game table with his greying elders.

Jane Obviously, Mr Lefroy sees little else to tempt him.

Elizabeth Are you surprised? A woman weeping into her handkerchief cannot hope to inspire admiration in the opposite sex — let alone good sense in her own.

Jane I am utterly ridiculous. Spurned by my would-be partner, I stand here alone and dream up suitors for my heroine. I wish that I had never taken up novel writing. There is nothing more ridiculous.

Elizabeth That is a rather insulting thing to say to a character from a novel.

Jane Oh. I beg your pardon. (*Pause*) Which character are you? And from which novel?

Elizabeth I have not yet made up my mind. For now, kindly cease your snivelling so that we may follow the exchange between these two gentlemen.

Jane Very well. I have no competing engagements.

Mr Bingley I would not be so fastidious as you for a kingdom, Darcy! Upon my honour, I never met with such pleasant company, or so many agreeable ladies. And accomplished, too.

Mr Darcy Accomplished?

Mr Bingley It is amazing to me how young ladies have the patience to be so very accomplished as they all are.

Mr Darcy All ladies accomplished?

Mr Bingley They all seem accomplished to me.

Mr Darcy I cannot boast of knowing more than half a dozen such women in the whole range of my acquaintance.

Elizabeth (*unheard by the gentlemen*) That man must comprehend a great deal in his idea of an accomplished woman. I suppose that a lady must have a thorough knowledge of music, singing, drawing, dancing, and the modern languages to deserve the word.

Mr Darcy To deserve the word, a lady must have a thorough knowledge of music, singing, drawing, dancing, and the modern languages.

Jane Does Mr Lefroy also seek such a woman?

Elizabeth If he does, then he deserves to find her, for she is certain to be insufferable.

Mr Darcy And to all this she must yet add something more substantial, in the improvement of her mind by extensive reading.

Elizabeth All these attributes united? In that case, I am no longer surprised at his knowing only six accomplished women. I rather wonder now at his knowing any.

Jane Miss, your tongue is quick. But you would not be so gay if you were slighted by a gentleman of consequence.

Elizabeth Is that so?

Jane Suppose my Mr Darcy were to put you to the test.

Elizabeth I should like to see him try.

Mr Bingley Well, whether the ladies at this ball are accomplished or not, you cannot deny that they are uncommonly pretty. (*He indicates Elizabeth*) Look! Here stands a lady in want of a partner. She is very pretty and, I dare say, very agreeable.

Jane Mr Darcy, do your worst.

Mr Darcy Which lady do you mean? (*He turns a critical eye to Elizabeth*) Oh. She is tolerable.

Elizabeth Tolerable?

Mr Darcy But not handsome enough to tempt me. I am in no humour at present to give consequence to young ladies who are slighted by other men.

Elizabeth Is that so?

Jane You see. It is not so pleasant to be snubbed.

Elizabeth As Mr Darcy is about to discover. (*She approaches Mr Darcy*) Dear sir, pray do not admit that I am tolerable. Make no such concession.

Jane Oh!

Mr Bingley Oh dear.

Elizabeth Were I to believe myself worthy of being tolerated by a Mr Darcy, the compliment would turn my head. I might even begin to aspire to dancing with the first valet to Mr Darcy's second footman. And what an insult that would be to the house of ... the house of ...?

Jane (*constructing the story as she speaks*) Pemberley. The house of Pemberley, in Derbyshire. Mr Darcy is the master of Pemberley, with an income of nine . . . no, ten thousand pounds a year.

Elizabeth Perhaps he should invest some of his prodigious income in lessons on manners.

Mr Darcy You expect me to be mortified, and to stammer a retraction. But why should I apologize to you for remarks spoken in confidence to another?

Elizabeth Why do you make confidential remarks where you are bound to be overheard?

Mr Darcy My meaning was that I never dance unless I am particularly acquainted with my partner.

Mr Bingley I can vouch for that. I have known Darcy to sit out dozens of dances because no lady of his acquaintance was present.

Elizabeth And of course, no one can ever become acquainted at a ball.

Mr Darcy Acquainted, perhaps, if to be acquainted is to ascertain that we agree that the weather is uncommonly seasonable for this time of year, or to talk entertainingly of Kent and Hertfordshire, of travelling and staying at home. For my part, I cannot consider myself to be properly acquainted with a lady unless we have thoroughly exchanged our views on books —

Elizabeth I am sure we never read the same, or not with the same feelings.

Mr Darcy As well as music —

Elizabeth I do not lay claim to any superior technique at my keyboard.

Mr Darcy And we must also have discussed —

Elizabeth Yes?

Mr Darcy In truth, what is of primary importance is not the subject matter, but rather, the manner in which it is discussed. There is a certain sort of lady who will treat every subject as an object of mockery or derision.

Elizabeth A certain sort of lady?

Mr Darcy A certain sort of unmarried lady. Unmarried and, I dare say, unmarriageable to any serious man.

Jane Oh!

Elizabeth Unmarried and, I dare say, determined to remain in that state until she finds a man who warrants her serious attention. Until then, she makes no apology for laughing at follies and nonsense whenever she can.

Jane Bravo! Bravo!

Mr Bingley I so dislike arguments. If you would conclude yours, I shall be very thankful.

Elizabeth What you ask is no sacrifice on my side. The moon is full, the music is lively, and the night is short. Miss Austen, if your Mr Darcy will not dance, I have no further use for him.

Mr Bingley We had better join the game table, Darcy.

Mr Darcy bows and repairs to the game table with Mr Bingley

Elizabeth Impossible man! Intolerable man!

Jane But he could not humble you, while I allowed Mr Lefroy to reduce me to tears. Bravo to you! From now on, I will make you my model, Miss — Miss — But who are you? You could be one of my heroine's neighbours. Or one of her sisters. But which? You are too sensible to be Lydia, and you are no peevish Kitty or bookish Mary.

Elizabeth Lydia, Kitty, and Mary. Are any of them proper companions for your heroine?

Jane The Bennet sisters provide comedy, not companionship. They are a rather silly trio.

Elizabeth How lonely your heroine must be.

Jane I had not thought of that. A woman experiencing her first love ought to have a dependable sister for confidences by candlelight. Do you volunteer for the role?

Elizabeth If I am to be a sister, I must be a younger sister. Too much is expected of the eldest.

Jane Jane Bennet will be your senior by a year. I am delighted to form your acquaintance, Miss ——

Elizabeth Elizabeth.

Jane Miss Elizabeth Bennet.

Elizabeth You may call me Lizzy.

Jane And you must call me Jane. So there are five Bennet sisters. . . Five unprovided-for Bennet sisters at that. The whole lot of you are doomed to poverty and want unless you find suitable husbands. Your father's estate will be entailed away to a distant cousin upon his death, you see.

Elizabeth You might have warned me of my incipient ruin before I agreed to join the Bennet family.

Jane We have that in common, you and I, the threat of a destitute and miserable old age. Never mind. What fun we will have in the meantime. My sweet heroine requires a sister with spirit.

Elizabeth I shall enjoy being a heroine's confidante.

Jane You do not begrudge your sister her leading role?

Elizabeth It is such a terrible responsibility to be a heroine, always setting an example. A heroine's sister can make an appearance when a scene wants enlivening. But no one misses her if she disappears on a solitary ramble on a rainy afternoon and returns three chapters later, her petticoats splattered with mud.

Jane Petticoats splattered with mud — I must make a note of that. (*She retrieves a small notebook and pencil from her reticule and jots down a note)*

Music begins. Harris approaches

Jane Oh dear.
Elizabeth What is it?
Jane The heir to this fine house. Hide me!
Elizabeth Is a lad of fourteen such a menace?
Jane Harris Bigg-Wither is fifteen to be precise, and most determined.
Harris Miss Austen!
Jane Master Bigg-Wither.
Harris You promised me a dance.
Jane Well remembered, sir.

Harris leads Jane downstage. They dance awkwardly during the ensuing interchange

Harris I shall marry you when I am twenty-one. See if I shan't.
Jane Sir, you speak with great authority on the subject.
Harris I told my sister that I shall marry you, and she said that it was a very good idea.
Jane (*amused*) Did she?
Harris "I am sure that Parson Austen's daughter never dreamed of becoming the mistress of such a house as this." That is what Alethea said.
Jane (*somewhat dismayed*) Did she?
Harris Then she said, "It would be such a relief for all of us to see Miss Jane Austen well settled."
Jane It is your turn to lead down the middle.
Harris Oh bother. (*He hastily executes the move*) And I said to Alethea that when you become my wife, you will fetch my slippers for me every night.
Jane To be sure, you deserve no less. But here, I have a confession to make. I have a dreadful habit of misplacing slippers and that sort of thing.
Harris I will keep my slippers under my bed, and you will always know where to find them.

The music ends

Since we are to be married, we must dance the next set.

Tom rises

Elizabeth Look! Mr Lefroy! Like Lazarus.

Tom approaches the others

Jane I shall not be the first to speak.

Tom makes a move to speak to Jane. She makes herself unapproachable. He changes tack, and addresses Harris

Tom Master Bigg-Wither, does Miss Austen monopolize your attention, causing you to neglect your other guests?

Harris No. I ——

Tom I know how difficult it is to tear oneself away from a fine pair of eyes in the face of a pretty woman. And so, to assist you, I volunteer to escort Miss Austen in the next set. That is, if the lady does not object.

Jane If you insist, sir. For Master Bigg-Wither's sake.

Harris Miss Austen was to dance with me!

Jane Be consoled, Harris. I may dance with others, but I shall always remember where you keep your bedroom slippers.

Harris We should never have invited strangers to our ball. I told Alethea as much.

Harris retreats to the card table

Tom (*with mock seriousness*) Miss Austen, I must inform you that a report of a most serious and alarming nature is circulating. A report with you as its subject.

Jane (*disorientated*) What sort of report, Mr Lefroy?

Tom A report so scandalous that I must have it contradicted at once.

Jane I cannot think ——

Tom I am told that you are writing a theatrical to be performed next week.

Jane Only a short sketch.

Tom I could not believe that you would engage in such frivolity ——

Jane A wintertime lark. Our custom at this time of year.

Tom I could not believe that you would engage in such unseemly frivolity . . . without offering me a role.

Jane I should have guessed what you were after!

Tom Now tell me. Who am I to play?

Jane Judging by your performance this evening, you will play the rheumatic grandfather hunched over the game table.

Tom Judging by my plight this evening, I should play the wounded swain who consoles himself with victories at cards for losses on the dance floor. I did not realize that I had a rival in young Master Bigg-Wither.

Elizabeth Many things escape a gentleman's attention when he fixes it to the game table.

Jane Indeed!

Tom (*playfully*) This is not to be endured. I must challenge Master Bigg-Wither to a duel.

Jane The swain would slaughter his rival?

Tom Does he have a choice?

Jane Is there no other way to appease his pride?

Tom None that I can think of . . . unless . . . unless the lady were to tender evidence that the swain is her preferred contender.

Jane What evidence would suffice?

Tom Were the swain less of a gentleman, he might suggest such means as would make a lady blush.

Jane But the swain is a gentleman.

Tom And as he is a gentleman, the lady would have no reason to deny him ——

Tom and Jane are about to kiss, then break away

— a lock of her hair.

Mrs Austen enters

Mrs Austen What a chill there is in the ballroom this evening.

Jane Is there, Mamma? I had not noticed.

Mrs Austen With the party thinning out, there is. I had no business going out at all tonight, let alone staying up until all hours. Mr Landers said so. "With joints like yours," he said, "the only thing to do is to stay at home with a cup of nettle tea."

Jane How could you think of staying at home on a night like this?

Mrs Austen I think it a very dull party.

Jane After the next dance, I will sit with you.

Mrs Austen It is time for us to go.

Jane But guests are still arriving.

Mrs Austen Have you no consideration for my joints?

Jane What will Miss Alethea think?

Mrs Austen I will make our excuses.

Jane Mamma!

Mrs Austen Now, Jane.

Jane Mamma, I am engaged to Mr Lefroy!

Mrs Austen (*all attention*) Engaged?

Jane Engaged to dance with Mr Lefroy, Mamma!

Mrs Austen Oh. Engaged to dance yet again with Mr Lefroy.

Elizabeth If invitations to dance are issued, the recipient is not to blame.

Jane (*to Elizabeth*) Yes!

Mrs Austen Everyone talks of how you behaved together at the Heartleys'.

Elizabeth Then your mamma's coming here to disrupt the dance will confirm their most scandalous conjectures.

Jane (*to Elizabeth*) If only I dared say that to Mamma!

Mrs Austen That fellow from Dublin is barely known to the neighbourhood.

Jane He is Madame Lefroy's nephew. And her guest. What more is required?

Mrs Austen Only that which you, yourself, lack.

Jane Fortune. (*With a touch of melodrama*) Our shared penury facilitates our mutual understanding. And so, I would not exchange my situation for an estate of forty thousand pounds.

Mrs Austen Some men might consider forty thousand pounds a most happy alternative to mutual understanding.

Jane You need not worry about money, Mamma. Mr Lefroy is the favourite of his relatives. They will see to everything.

Mrs Austen Provided that he remains their favourite. What do you think Madame Lefroy makes of your friendship?

Jane Why should she not be pleased? A woman in such easy circumstances as Madame Lefroy must be indifferent to wealth.

Mrs Austen A woman does not attain Madame Lefroy's easy circumstances unless she is highly partial to wealth. Jane, fetch your cloak.

Jane Now?

Mrs Austen Now.

Jane (*to Elizabeth*) How infuriating, to be ordered home by one's mother.

Elizabeth How humiliating to submit to such orders.

Jane What alternative do I have?

Elizabeth What alternative have you the spirit to devise?

Madame Lefroy rises from the game table and approaches

Jane (*inspired*) Of course! Look, Mamma! Madame Lefroy! Good-evening, Madame Lefroy!

Madame Lefroy Mrs Austen! Jane!

Jane Madame Lefroy, tell us! Have you decided to engage the young parson who visited you last week?

Madame Lefroy I certainly have. I was entirely delighted with our first interview. What a deferential young clergyman, and so eager to please! He is just the sort of respectful, humble young man that one never encounters anymore.

Elizabeth If one is lucky.

Mrs Austen (*pointedly*) There are entirely too many of the other sort about.

Jane The dance is about to begin, but I know that Mamma will insist on knowing all.

Mrs Austen We dine with you tomorrow. We can discuss your meeting at dinner.

Jane Impossible! You must relate all the particulars to Mamma tonight, so that she can give me a faithful account of them on our way home.

Madame Lefroy We matrons will find a breezy corner in which to confer while you young people dance. It is far too warm here.

Mrs Austen Of course. (*To Jane*) Your sister would never behave like this.

Mrs Austen and Madame Lefroy separate from the others and seat themselves by the game table, UL

Tom Do not suppose, Miss Austen, that your mother's interruption has distracted the swain from his suit. (*Touching Jane's hair*) Unless the lady tenders her evidence, the duel must be fought.

Jane How dreadful ... (*To Elizabeth*) Lizzy, have you a pair of scissors?

Elizabeth Perhaps.

Jane I must have them.

Elizabeth Have you so many curls that one may be dispatched?

Jane It has been summoned to prevent a tragedy. Lizzy, please.

Elizabeth retrieves a small pair of scissors that was tucked into her sash, and hands them to Jane. Jane cuts a lock of her hair and a piece of ribbon from her costume. She tucks the scissors ino her sash and ties the ribbon around the lock of hair. Elizabeth assists so that the actions are fluid and rapid

Elizabeth And now that I have assisted you in every possible way, I suppose I am to be dismissed.

Jane Poor Lizzy, are you feeling deserted?

Elizabeth Never mind about me, Miss Austen. Now that I can be of no further use, you may leave me to entertain myself.

Jane Out of the question . . . I have the very partner for you!

Elizabeth You do?

Jane Oh yes. A young parson, in fact. Mr . . . Collins. Mr William Collins. (*She leads Harris downstage and transforms him into Mr Collins*) And he is just the sort of respectful, humble young man one never encounters any more. (*Moulding Mr Collins into a servile posture*) Quite out of the common way.

Mr Collins I always strive to compensate for the arrogance for which others of my sex are so justly chastized.

Jane Is that so, Mr Collins?

Mr Collins My estimable patroness is unequivocal in her censure of such men.

Jane And pray, who is your patroness?

Mr Collins Do not insult me by pretending that you have not heard speak of Lady Catherine de Bourgh, widow of the illustrious late Sir Lewis de Bourgh. He was a baronet.

Jane Lady Catherine . . . A charming lady, I am sure.

Elizabeth You offer me a most diverting companion.

Jane He should satisfy your taste for folly and nonsense. Mr Collins, Miss Elizabeth Bennet. Miss Bennet, Mr William Collins.

Mr Collins bows. Jane gestures for him to bow lower, and then lower

Elizabeth Mr Collins will not mind if I retreat to the sofa, for I know that the clergyman of so eminent a patroness would not think it proper to dance.

Mr Collins To the contrary, Miss Bennet, I am by no means of the opinion that a ball of this kind, given by an established family can have any evil tendency. And I am so far from objecting to dancing myself that I shall take this opportunity to solicit your hand. Perhaps you fear that I am accustomed to fine dancing at the home of Lady Catherine de Bourgh, and that this humble entertainment will not compare. Set your mind at ease and be assured that this evening, I come prepared to admire all that I see.

Jane How convenient. Even now, Lizzy confided to me that she is sorely in want of a partner. You must join Mr Lefroy and me as we require a second couple.

Mr Collins Delightful!

The music begins. Mr Collins leads Elizabeth to the dance space. Jane rejoins Tom, and the ensuing dance sequence reflects the dynamics of their flirtation

Tom Miss Austen is hiding something.

Jane (*showing Tom the lock of hair*) You refer, perhaps, to this?

Tom The persuasive evidence at last!

Jane It is the swain who shall have to be persuasive to obtain it.

Tom The swain depends upon generosity, not persuasion. The lady's generosity.

Jane Or foolishness.
Tom O, wilt thou leave me so unsatisfied?
Jane What satisfaction canst thou have tonight?
Tom That which might sustain an Irish Romeo when he is banished from this English Verona.
Jane Banished, Mr Lefroy?
Tom London is a sordid place. How is a man to withstand temptation amid the cock and hen clubs and the stews of Covent Garden? A token from his lady would steel his resolve.
Jane Can one lock of hair achieve so much?
Tom One lady can.
Jane If only the lady could be certain of the swain.
Tom Does the lady doubt her power to enchant?
Jane She no longer doubts his power to persuade. (*She presents the lock of hair to Tom*)

The music ends

Mr Collins bows to Elizabeth, steps away, and is transformed into Harris

Harris Did you see what Miss Austen did?
Mrs Austen Did anyone fail to see what my daughter did?
Madame Lefroy How difficult it must be for a girl without a dowry to find a good husband. Particularly a girl like Jane.
Harris I would slay that Mr Lefroy with my penknife, except that he is a guest at our ball.

Harris exits

Madame Lefroy Tom, may I speak to you?

Mrs Austen exits

Tom approaches Madame Lefroy and sits beside her at the game table

Jane Oh, Lizzy. What will my sister, Cassandra, say?
Elizabeth Nothing to any effect, now that the deed is done.
Jane Do not scold me, Lizzy. You are jealous of my dance partner.
Elizabeth I will own that my partner was not as bewitching as yours.
Jane If you mean to tease me, I know how to distract you. (*Calling to Mr Darcy*) Oh, Mr Darcy! Will you join our party?

Mr Darcy (*from his seat at the game table*) I must decline. I can imagine but two motives for your conferring like this. My joining you would interfere with either.

Jane Lizzy, can you understand his meaning?

Elizabeth Not at all, but depend upon it, he means to be severe on us.

Jane Mr Darcy, I demand an explanation.

Mr Darcy You either choose this method of passing the evening because you are in each other's confidence, and have secret affairs to discuss, or because you are conscious that you have chosen a position where your figures appear to the greatest advantage. If the first, I should be completely in your way, and if the second, I can admire you much better from here.

Jane Shocking! How shall we punish Mr Darcy for such a speech, Lizzy?

Elizabeth Tease him. Laugh at him.

Jane Or worse yet, force him to gaze with interest — no, with admiration — precisely where he is most determined to find fault.

Mr Darcy looks at Elizabeth, looks away and looks at her again

Reel music begins

Mr Darcy approaches Jane and Elizabeth

Mr Darcy Do you not feel a great inclination, Miss Bennet, to seize this opportunity to dance a reel?

Pause

I said, Miss Bennet ——

Elizabeth I heard you before. But I could not immediately determine what to say in reply. You wanted me to say "Yes," that you might have the pleasure of despising my taste. I have therefore made up my mind to tell you that I do not want to dance a reel at all — and now despise me if you dare.

Mr Darcy Indeed, I do not dare.

Mr Darcy exits

Music fades

Jane What a remarkable woman I am making of you, Lizzy.

Elizabeth Unbearable man!

Jane But well spoken ... and rather handsome.

Pause

Jane Lizzy, do you think that Mr Lefroy will ask me to dance again? I must make the most of the evening, for you may be sure that Mamma's joints will be insufferable in the morning. (*Mimicking Mrs Austen*) "Oh, my joints. Mr Lander's nettle tea might as well be poison for all the good it does."

Madame Lefroy and Elizabeth exit

Black-out. If stage is already set for Scene 2, lights crossfade to the Austens' parlour, UR

SCENE 2

The following morning. The parlour at the Austen home

The space is furnished with three chairs. The chair on the right is placed by a writing desk equipped with a notebook (Jane's manuscript), pens, paper and an inkwell. Next to the other chairs, UL*, there is a pile of garments for mending and a workbasket. Mrs Austen enters. Her first line overlaps with the end of Jane's speech in Scene 1*

Mrs Austen Oh, my joints. Mr Lander's nettle tea might as well be poison for all the good it does.

Jane either moves from the ballroom to the parlour, or enters L. *She removes her shawl while crossing the stage to the writing desk, and adds it to the mending pile by the workbasket. Jane may move the writing desk and chair downstage. She sits at the writing desk*

Jane (*composing a letter*) "My dear Cassandra, we had an exceedingly good ball last night. You scold me so much in the nice, long letter which I have received from you that I am almost afraid to tell you how my Irish friend and I behaved. Imagine to yourself everything most profligate and shocking." (*She sets down her pen and rises from the desk*) When Mamma and I visit his aunt for dinner this afternoon, I shall think myself very ill-used if Mr Lefroy is not seated by me. How could Madame Lefroy have set the dinner hour so late? It was done to test my patience.

Mrs Austen Five o'clock is far too early for dinner. What was Madame Lefroy thinking?

Jane She usually invites her guests for four.

Mrs Austen I shall never finish all the mending by then.

Jane Let me help you, Mamma.

Mrs Austen I am of half of a mind to write to Madame Lefroy this instant to send our apologies for this afternoon.

Jane No!

Mrs Austen How else are we to finish the mending?

Jane If one always insisted on finishing the mending before going out, one should never be seen in company from one season to the next.

Mrs Austen It would be better never to be seen than always to make a spectacle of one's self. (*She proceeds to the writing desk, sits down and begins a letter*) "Saturday, January the ninth. Dear Madame Lefroy —— "

Jane What are you doing?

Mrs Austen (*writing*) "It was a pleasure to converse with you last night. Imagine my disappointment, this morning, to find that I am indisposed."

Jane Mamma! Please!

Mrs Austen "Therefore, I am afraid that it will be necessary for us to cancel our engagement."

Jane No!

Mrs Austen You are too giddy for company.

Elizabeth enters

Elizabeth Henceforth only the sober and stony-faced are to be allowed out of doors.

Jane Lizzy!

Mrs Austen You should not be out at all with Cassandra away.

Elizabeth I think it very hard upon a younger sister to be denied her share of society because the elder visits her friends.

Jane (*to Elizabeth*) Yes! (*To Mrs Austen*) Surely the last born has as good a right to the pleasures of youth as the first.

Mrs Austen You want your sister to steady you. I am not up to the task.

Jane Mr Lefroy leaves for Lincoln's Inn next week. Barely any time remains.

Mrs Austen (*writing*) "Please accept my sincere apologies, and Jane's as well. Affectionately yours —— "

Jane (*to Elizabeth*) There is no swaying Mamma.

Elizabeth So long as her daughter is easily swayed.

Jane But Mamma is determined to stay home.

Elizabeth Is her daughter not determined to go out?

Jane Without her? What will Madame Lefroy say if I appear unaccompanied?

Elizabeth How will you feel if you do not appear at all?

Jane Mamma, I am very sorry that your joints plague you this morning. But you must be equally pleased that mine are in good working order.

Mrs Austen Yes ——

Jane And therefore, I am sure you will agree that your decision to break an engagement does not necessitate my doing the same.

Mrs Austen You can hardly go without me.

Jane I am familiar with the route.

Mrs Austen What will Madame Lefroy say if you appear unaccompanied?

Elizabeth Just think, Jane! You will be quite the spectacle!

Jane (*to Mrs Austen*) I will be quite the spectacle, standing alone at her threshold, my petticoats splattered with mud — no chaperone to remind me to sidestep the puddles, you see!

Elizabeth What an embarrassment for your family!

Jane (*to Mrs Austen*) I own that such conduct will not reflect so very well upon my Mamma.

Elizabeth Particularly if you should happen to confess to Madame Lefroy ——

Jane (*to Mrs Austen*) Particularly if I should happen to drop a hint that my mamma rather exaggerated her indisposition because she fancied staying home to do the mending.

Pause

Mrs Austen (*putting down her pen*) If we are to walk to the Lefroys, I must take a draught of nettle tea. I do not know what has come over you, Jane.

Jane I will finish the sewing while you drink your tea. (*She takes a needle and thread from the workbasket and begins to mend a garment from the pile*)

Mrs Austen You are not wealthy enough to be so wilful.

Mrs Austen exits

Elizabeth You have a determined spirit, Jane. I hope you have found a gentleman who shares it.

Jane He certainly was resolved to gain his prize last night. (*She returns to the writing desk, taking her needlework with her, sets down her needlework and takes notes in her notebook during her ensuing* *conversation with Elizabeth*) Now tell me, Lizzy, after the ball, did your sister speak to you of Mr Bingley? Is my Jane Bennet greatly charmed by her new admirer?

Elizabeth My sister tells me that she has never seen such happy manners in a gentleman.

Jane That is promising.

Elizabeth And she smiles quietly when I observe that he is also handsome, which a young man ought likewise to be, if he possibly can.

Jane Well said, Lizzy! With you as Jane Bennet's confidante, my novel could really be something. Your mother must be boasting to all her neighbours that Mr Bingley will propose to Jane within a fortnight.

Elizabeth Mamma is incapable of fatigue when enumerating the advantages of the match.

Jane And Kitty and Lydia are already dreaming of the balls to be hosted by Mrs Jane Bingley.

Elizabeth I wish they would hold their tongues, in public at least.

Jane So all are agreed that Mr Bingley and your sister will be a perfectly delightful couple, and that I was very clever to have introduced them to one another.

Elizabeth Too clever, perhaps.

Jane What do you mean?

Elizabeth It is evident to everyone that Mr Bingley and my sister will be married by spring. How will you fill three volumes with their story?

Jane Rest assured. Great obstacles will beset them.

Elizabeth Such as?

Jane Well, first —

Elizabeth Yes?

Jane First ... First ... Shame on you for making me doubt myself! (*She resumes her sewing*) If you are determined to thwart my novel, come and help me finish the mending, for I may soon find myself in a great hurry to sew a night-gown for my wedding night.

Elizabeth You are confident, then, of a certain gentleman's feelings?

Jane How we shall laugh at Mamma's scruples when I am Mrs Tom Lefroy. (*Setting down her needlework and returning to her writing*) I must continue with my story, for I am determined to finish a novel before I marry. I must set down your exchange with Mr Collins. (*Writing in her notebook*) "Elizabeth asked Mr Collins whether he would think it proper to join in the evening's amusement and was surprised to find that he entertained no scruple. 'To the contrary, Miss Elizabeth, I am by no means of the opinion that a ball of this kind, given by an established family can have any evil tendency — ' "

Elizabeth I am glad that my humiliation last night continues to afford you such pleasure.

Jane Lizzy, I am such a vain, selfish creature that I would subject you to all manner of torment for the sake of comedy. I must see a book in print before I marry. And when a thousand copies are sold, I will take a carriage to the best warehouses in London, and fill my wedding chest. And everyone will wonder how Parson Austen's younger daughter can afford such luxuries.

Elizabeth Be careful, or Mr Lefroy will expect you to supply your own pin money by the same method.

Jane What ideas you have, Lizzy. When Miss Jane Austen becomes Mrs Tom Lefroy, she will set aside her pen.

Elizabeth Very likely.

Jane How is Mrs Lefroy to write novels with a household to manage?

Elizabeth How is Mrs Lefroy to manage a household with novels to write?

Jane Mr Lefroy means to be chief justice of Ireland.

Elizabeth How long, I wonder, before Mrs Chief Justice of Ireland creeps downstairs in the dead of night, candle in hand, to unlock her writing desk?

Jane Is that what you imagine?

Elizabeth She will write in a room with a squeaking door to warn her of sudden intruders.

Jane shakes her head and scoffs

She will pen her novels into notebooks, or on to tiny slips of paper —

Jane (*sarcastically*) While pretending to attend to her correspondence.

Elizabeth A male relation will send her novels to a publisher, and negotiate the sale.

Jane (*drawn into Elizabeth's fantasy despite herself*) Publication must be anonymous. And if I am to write, I must have critical acclaim as well as popularity.

Elizabeth Instant success, of course. Glowing praise in the Quarterly Review.

Jane And a nation of adoring readers.

Elizabeth Everyone speculates as to the identity of the anonymous lady writer.

Jane But my secret remains protected.

Elizabeth For a while, perhaps. But sooner or later word gets out that Jane Austen is an author.

Jane Jane Austen is an author. (*Pause*) Lizzy, how you carry on. Why should Mrs Tom Lefroy wish to write? She will have no need for invention. Her own home will furnish everything she desires.

Elizabeth Everything but a writing desk.
Jane Lizzy, when you decide to marry, you will understand.
Elizabeth I challenge my dear author to create a suitable suitor.
Jane It is not so amusing to create suitable suitors as it is to create the other kind. Where can Mr Darcy be keeping himself this morning?
Elizabeth (*protesting*) Jane!
Jane (*calling*) Oh Mr Darcy!
Elizabeth No!

Mr Darcy strides onstage, all energy. He hands his gloves and hat peremptorily to Jane, who places them out of sight, behind the mending pile

Mr Darcy In vain have I struggled. It will not do. I must tell you how ardently I admire and love you.
Jane Oh!
Mr Darcy The depth of my feelings cannot be doubted.
Jane One could almost forgive him his vanity.
Mr Darcy For they have rooted themselves in my breast despite your connections, despite your relations, despite everything.
Jane Almost.
Mr Darcy I told myself that I could not inflict such an alliance upon my family. I sought to be ruled by my duty. I considered your relations and your situation in life, and tried to deny or ignore all that I felt. But your charm has overwhelmed my will and my judgment. And I hope that the strength of my attachment will now be rewarded by your acceptance of my hand.
Jane Well, Lizzy, you cannot be insensible to the compliment of such a man's affections, although his mode of declaring them is somewhat frank.
Elizabeth Let frankness be the order of the day. Mr Darcy, in such cases at this, it is the established mode to express a sense of obligation for the sentiments avowed, however unequally they may be returned. If I could feel gratitude, I would now thank you. But I cannot. I have never desired your good opinion, and you have bestowed it most unwillingly. The feelings which initially prevented the acknowledgment of your regard can have little difficulty in overcoming it now.
Mr Darcy And this is your reply! I might perhaps wish to be informed why, with so little endeavour at civility, I am thus rejected. But it is of small importance.
Elizabeth I might as well enquire why, with so evident a design of offending me, you tell me that you like me against your will?
Mr Darcy The feelings I related are natural and just.

Elizabeth What precisely sets a Bennet so far below a Darcy? You are a gentleman. I am a gentleman's daughter. So far, we are equal.

Mr Darcy Consider, Miss Bennet, the vulgarity displayed by your mother and the want of propriety displayed by your younger sisters. Was I to rejoice in the prospect of such connections? And even if these scruples could be overcome, what sort of a wife would Miss Elizabeth Bennet make for the man who governs Pemberley?

Elizabeth You are right, Mr Darcy. We are not equal. I am a gentleman's daughter, while you are no gentleman. And you are the last man in the world whom I could ever be prevailed upon to marry. Jane, you will regret this.

Elizabeth seizes the notebook. Jane begins to chase her around the stage. Elizabeth is initially annoyed, but both women are soon carried away by the hilarity of the moment

Mrs Austen enters holding a letter. She observes Jane for a moment

Mrs Austen Jane?

Jane Mamma! I was searching for my needle.

Mr Darcy (*to Mrs Austen*) I require my gloves and hat.

Jane (*pretending to find her needle*) Oh, look! Here it is.

Mr Darcy I said, I require my gloves and hat. The service in this house is intolerable.

Jane You are addressing my mother, Mr Darcy, not a servant!

Mrs Austen A letter has come for you, Jane.

Jane takes the letter from her mother

Jane From Madame Lefroy! (*She opens the letter, and reads it out loud*) "My dear Jane, It was a pleasure to converse with you yesterday. Imagine my disappointment, this morning, to find that I am indisposed. Therefore, I am afraid that it will be necessary for me to cancel our engagement. Please accept my sincere apologies, and convey them to your mother, as well. Affectionately yours, Madame Lefroy." (*Pause*) There will be ample time for the mending after all, Mamma.

Mrs Austen Fancy. Perhaps Madame Lefroy should try Mr Landers' nettle tea.

Mrs Austen exits

Elizabeth How vexed you must be.

Jane There is more to the letter. I would not have read the postscript to Mamma for the world. Madame Lefroy writes that upon further reflection ——

Elizabeth (*reading over Jane's shoulder*)—"it would be prudent to postpone any communication between our houses for a week."

Jane Mr Lefroy leaves for London next Saturday!

Elizabeth (*reading*) "I trust you will not mistake my meaning. Yours sincerely, Madame Lefroy."

Jane Was this written at Mr Lefroy's request? Has he reconsidered his feelings?

Elizabeth Do you think it likely? Consult your judgment.

Jane I fear that is precisely what has occurred.

Elizabeth There is another possibility.

Jane I cannot think of one.

Elizabeth I can. Will you hear it?

Jane Gladly.

Elizabeth Madame Lefroy sees that her nephew is in love with you and does not approve of his choice.

Jane But Madame Lefroy has always wished to see me well settled.

Lady Catherine enters

Lady Catherine There is a world of difference between a girl whom one wishes to see well settled and a future niece. An aunt cannot be too careful in supervising her nephew's choices. I shall instruct my parson, Mr Collins, to include a few thoughts on the subject in his next sermon.

Jane Lady Catherine? Lady Catherine de Bourgh? (*She curtsies*)

Lady Catherine I can see by your curtsey that you have not had the benefit of a proper governess. If I had known your mother, I should have admonished her to engage one. Yes, I can see quite clearly that there are many reasons for an aunt to steer her nephew out of your reach.

Elizabeth And many more reasons for a nephew to steer himself out of yours.

Lady Catherine Your impertinence does not escape me, Miss. A nephew brought up to respect his aunt will welcome, and even solicit her advice. Why in the case of my Fitzwilliam—(*she notices Mr Darcy*) Fitzwilliam!

Mr Darcy Good-morning, Aunt Catherine.

Lady Catherine I hardly expected to find you in such company. I am not accustomed to surprises.

Jane So Mr Darcy is Lady Catherine's nephew.

Elizabeth I thought I detected a family resemblance.

Lady Catherine I only condescended to make a visit because I was passing by with my daughter to take some air. My daughter waits for me outside in our carriage. Fitzwilliam, you will join us.

Mr Darcy You must excuse me, Aunt Catherine, but I have matters to attend to. And I am waiting for my hat.

Lady Catherine Then you must visit us soon. You will find my daughter more radiant then ever. She grows particularly refined from spending so many hours indoors. Delicacy requires her to keep her distance from other ladies. So says my new parson, Mr Collins, a most invaluable servant.

Lady Catherine exits

Elizabeth I hardly know which is the more ridiculous of the two, the parson or his patroness.

Jane Lady Catherine will do well for my novel. But suppose that Madame Lefroy shares her views?

Elizabeth I hope that your happiness depends on the views of the nephew and not the aunt.

Jane Madame Lefroy may believe that in separating us, she does a kindness to her nephew. (*Pause*) Who can inflict greater damage than a well meaning relation . . . or friend? Of course!

Elizabeth What is it, Jane?

Jane That is the obstacle. The obstacle that will come between Jane Bennet and Mr Bingley. The contrivances of a well-intentioned companion.

Elizabeth Who would seek to separate Mr Bingley from my sister?

Jane nods at Mr Darcy

Do you fancy Mr Bingley too fine for Miss Jane Bennet, Mr Darcy?

Mr Darcy There are many objections to the match.

Elizabeth Those same objections did not prevent you from soliciting my hand, not half an hour ago.

Mr Darcy Towards my friend I will be kinder than I have been towards myself.

Elizabeth Mr Bingley's attachment is too strong. Your efforts will fail.

Mr Darcy I rarely fail when I apply my effort to my duty. You may wish to prepare your sister for disappointment. But I imagine that her regret will be superficial, for I have seen that the hearts of the Bennet sisters are not easily touched.

Elizabeth Jane, I cannot bear the sight of this man any longer.

Jane retrieves Mr Darcy's gloves from behind the mending pile and hands them to him

Jane Mr Darcy, you were waiting for these.
Elizabeth And this. (*She takes Mr Darcy's hat and sets it on his head*)

Mr Darcy exits

My poor sister.
Jane Miss Jane Bennet has nothing to fear. She is the heroine of a novel. All her problems will resolve themselves by the end of volume three. (*Pause*) Would that Miss Jane Austen had similar assurance.

Elizabeth squeezes Jane's hand affectionately

Elizabeth Jane, you must allow Mr Lefroy to prove himself. Now practise your sewing for your night-gown.
Jane When a woman must wait, what is there for her to do, but sew?

The doorbell rings

Tom (*off*) I will wait for her in the parlour.

Tom enters

Miss Austen!
Jane Mr Lefroy!
Tom The maid said that she would fetch you. But here you are.
Jane Is your aunt recovered?
Tom Somewhat.
Jane Madame Lefroy is favoured with a robust constitution.
Tom Nonetheless, for the moment, she remains unable to entertain guests.
Jane How vexing. That is, poor Madame Lefroy.
Tom Her timing is particularly unfortunate, for I have been instructed to pack my trunks. My departure to London has been accelerated.
Jane When do we lose your company, Mr Lefroy?
Tom The day after tomorrow.
Jane So soon?
Tom I must renounce my part in your theatrical, and many other anticipated pleasures besides. My great-uncle wishes for me to begin my studies directly.
Jane You are most attentive to your great-uncle's wishes.

Tom A nephew must be attentive to the wishes of a great-uncle who pays for his education. Particularly if the nephew has a mother and sisters to provide for in the years ahead. Unfortunately, the great-uncle of an attentive nephew is liable to form wishes on any number of topics.

Jane Such as?

Tom (*gravely*) To begin with ... (*His tone shifts to playfulness*) The uncle scrutinizes his nephew's reading lists, and monitors his attendance at lessons.

Jane (*trying to rally her spirits*) I suppose that even the nephew's choice of newspaper is dictated by his elder.

Tom The nephew must report daily on his diet, his employments, and his mode of exercise.

Jane Every morning, he must submit the proposed route of his walk for review and approval.

Tom His appearance is inspected from head to foot before he dares step out of doors.

Jane Laughter is prohibited between the hours of eight in the morning and seven at night.

Tom His leisure must be devoted entirely to "improving" activities.

Jane And his companions must all be sombre, sober fellows.

Tom Sombre, sober fellows every one ... (*Growing serious*) And fellows of great consequence if the nephew is to pay their sisters any mind.

Jane Is that so, Mr Lefroy?

Tom My uncle means well. But he believes that the purpose of matrimony is to consolidate wealth.

Elizabeth I thought that the purpose of wealth was to facilitate matrimony — with the partner of one's choice.

Tom My aunt appears to agree with him.

Jane And so, this morning, she was disposed to be indisposed.

Tom What would Miss Austen advise such a nephew?

Jane Does the nephew lack for advisors?

Tom To deserve his lady, he must make his way in the world. To make his way, he must desert his lady.

Jane The nephew has no ally?

Tom His family is of one mind.

Jane And quite decided?

Tom The nephew can only hope that some day, circumstances will permit him to resume his suit for the lady's hand.

Jane (*wistfully*) Some day ...

Elizabeth Some day? For shame!

Jane Am I to renounce all hope?

Elizabeth Would you cling to hope without commitment?

Jane What commitment is Mr Lefroy at liberty to give?
Elizabeth One that accords with his will.
Jane Would you have him cross his relations?
Elizabeth If needs be. But why should he not win them over? What of the future barrister's vaunted power of persuasion?
Tom Miss Austen, I can see that you desire my absence.
Elizabeth Speak to him, Jane.
Jane Mr Lefroy —
Tom Miss Austen?
Jane You asked me how I would advise the dutiful nephew of the opinionated uncle.
Tom You did not answer.
Jane Tell him this from me. Tell him that, upon reflection, I cannot believe that a gentleman of his stamp —
Elizabeth — a gentleman who is adept at recommending himself to others —
Jane — a gentleman with his talent for making friends, should have to choose between his heart and his prospects. There must be some avenue. There must be some solution.
Tom I have been walking about the laneways for hours, trying to think of one.
Jane There must be a solution because —
Elizabeth — because nothing can be worse than forsaking one's love.
Jane — because nothing can be worse than forsaking one's love — (*impulsively*) except to return that love, and to be the one who is forsaken.
Elizabeth What a remarkable woman I am making of you, Jane.
Tom Miss Austen, you are a remarkable woman.
Jane If I am, I cannot help it.
Tom You would have me, then?
Jane I would not have another.
Tom Even under these circumstances?
Jane Can you doubt it?
Tom Miss Jane Austen is not to be doubted.
Jane Mr Lefroy!
Tom Miss Austen! Jane! Dear, darling Jane!
Jane Tom, we are to be the happiest couple in the world.
Tom I will leave Hampshire with a heart lighter than air.
Jane Lizzy, did I not tell you that Tom would prove himself? I hope your needle and thread are at the ready. A night-gown is in order, and a good deal of fresh linen besides.

Lady Catherine enters

Lady Catherine Linen? Night-gowns? You talk as though you were about to be married.
Elizabeth Lady Catherine, it may please you to learn that Miss Austen is engaged.
Lady Catherine She is no such thing.
Elizabeth I assure you, she is. Mr Lefroy has asked for her hand.
Lady Catherine Oh. Is that all?
Jane All?
Lady Catherine A woman is engaged when her older relations, and his, have authorized the union.
Jane They will. Once we have a chance to tell them.
Lady Catherine So, your parents have not even been informed of your little scheme.
Jane It has only just transpired.
Lady Catherine And you believe yourself to be engaged.
Elizabeth Jane will tell them now.
Jane Now? Lizzy!
Elizabeth She will gain their blessing. You will see.
Jane Surely, it would be better to wait for the right moment?
Elizabeth What do you fear?
Jane Tom, I will fetch my parents.
Tom What for?
Jane Why, so that you may tell them!
Tom Tell them what?
Jane About our engagement, of course.
Tom You are not serious.
Jane Should we win over your uncle first? You must depart today to secure his blessing.
Tom Jane, we cannot tell him yet.
Jane Why not?
Tom Did you not hear me? All my prospects depend upon my uncle's good will.

Pause

Jane So, you propose a secret engagement?
Elizabeth Oh.
Tom Not forever, of course.
Jane For how long?
Tom Until my position is established.
Elizabeth Until then, he would subject his heart's object to the utmost uncertainty, himself to indefinite delay, and everyone to deceit?
Tom It cannot be any other way.

Elizabeth There is always another way.
Jane Yes. There is always another way.
Tom I am utterly dependent.
Jane But not without resources.
Tom What resources?

Mrs Austen enters, initially unseen by the others

Jane Have you so little confidence in your hold on your relations' affections?
Tom You really think they could be convinced?
Jane Did you not convince me?
Tom I suppose I did . . .
Jane Now claim me if you dare!
Mrs Austen You hesitate, Mr Lefroy. I suspect that, unlike my daughter, you are a realist.
Jane Mamma!
Tom Mrs Austen!
Elizabeth How dare your mother eavesdrop on your private conversation?
Lady Catherine In this age, a mother must use every means at her disposal.
Tom I hardly know what to say.
Elizabeth Is the future barrister at a loss for words?
Jane I am not. Give me courage, Lizzy. Mamma, we are to be married.
Mrs Austen Are you?
Jane Yes, we are.
Mrs Austen Have you lost your head?
Jane I have lost my heart. We both have. Neither of us can love another, and therefore, we must wed. You must give us your blessing, and all of our relations must drink a toast at our wedding breakfast.
Elizabeth Bravo! And again, bravo!

Pause. Tom claps his hands with assumed bravado

Tom Bravo, Miss Austen! Mrs Austen, you interrupted us at an opportune moment. We were rehearsing a scene from your daughter's new theatrical. How could she resist delivering an impromptu performance? Is she not a convincing actress? Bravo, and again bravo!
Mrs Austen My daughter will see you to the door, Mr Lefroy. Please tell your aunt that we hope she recovers soon. I know what it is to be troubled by one's health.

Jane and Tom separate from Mrs Austen

Jane Tom?

Tom Miss Austen, are you determined to ruin us both?

Jane What else could I do?

Tom There is only one thing for me to do. I know that now. On Saturday, I will leave for London to begin my studies. I have a mother and sisters to think of. They are too easily forgotten when I am in the company of a certain lady. And now, Miss Austen must excuse me. My aunt reminded me three times, this morning, to be punctual for dinner.

Jane Ever the dutiful nephew, Mr Lefroy.

Tom One more thing. I should return this token, which you so obligingly bestowed on me. (*He hands Jane the lock of hair*) Dear Jane, why did you not hold your tongue? We might yet have been husband and wife. Why could you not show some patience, some attention to the demands of the world? My aunt was right. "Even if she were an heiress, what sort of wife would Miss Austen make for a man who plans to become chief justice?" Good-day, Miss Austen.

Tom bows to Jane and exits

Jane tries unsuccessfully to rip the lock of hair apart, and then throws it across the room

Mrs Austen (*picking up the lock of hair*) Is our family so grand that we can afford to waste good ribbon at nine shillings and sixpence a yard?

Mrs Austen exits

Lady Catherine I always advise young ladies of modest means that waste is the most impermissible of all indulgences.

Jane Yes, Lady Catherine. Henceforth, I will practise exemplary economy.

Lady Catherine The virtue of making a small income go a good way cannot be overly prized. I will instruct my parson, Mr Collins, to make domestic economy the theme of his next sermon.

Mr Collins enters

Mr Collins Certainly, Your Ladyship.

Elizabeth Not him!

Lady Catherine If you require Christian counsel on this subject, Miss Austen, I recommend the services of my clergyman.

Mr Collins I, in turn, venture to hope that in carrying out her resolution, Miss Austen will draw upon such support as the church may humbly offer.

Elizabeth A bracing walk in the fresh air would do you more good.

Jane I have done taking your advice, Miss Elizabeth Bennet.

Elizabeth Jane, you were wonderful. You were brave and steadfast.

Jane And it brought me little joy. From now on, I mean to be cautious and reasonable.

Elizabeth I will not allow it.

Jane To the contrary. I will not allow you to lead me astray again. You want restraining.

Lady Catherine This case warrants the most severe restraint of all. Matrimony.

Mr Collins It is a man's most sacred duty to guide his wife with a firm hand.

Jane (*to Elizabeth*) Yes . . . You want a husband.

Lady Catherine turns to leave. Mr Collins prepares to follow her

Jane Stay, Mr Collins.

Mr Collins (*to Lady Catherine*) Your Ladyship?

Lady Catherine nods and exits

Jane Mr Collins, I must reconsider your role in my novel.

Elizabeth Whatever for?

Jane tears a sheet from her notebook, crumples it, and sets it aside. Elizabeth picks up the discarded sheet

Elizabeth My encounter with Mr Collins at the ballroom. Jane, what are you doing?

Jane It does not suit. I am starting afresh.

Elizabeth I will not allow you to throw the best of your work away. You take too much pride in it. (*She tucks the sheet of paper into her costume, e.g., her sash*)

Mr Collins Pride goeth before the fall. I say this despite the fact, and perhaps even because, there are certain ladies in this room who may not be unjustly rebuked of this vice.

Jane Mr Collins, I must ask you to abandon your absurd brand of pompous humility.

Mr Collins But it has taken me ever so long to master.

Jane It will no longer do.

Elizabeth Jane, put down your pen. Mr Collins is perfect as he was.

Jane (*to Mr Collins*) And while you are about it, please straighten your shoulders.

Mr Collins straightens his shoulders a little. Jane motions for him to straighten himself further.

You must be tired of stooping.

Mr Collins Lady Catherine prefers her servants to stand lower than herself.

Jane Have no fear. Your position with Lady Catherine is secure.

Mr Collins How can you be certain?

Jane I will arrange it. I mean to see Elizabeth comfortably settled. Domesticated, but not destitute.

Mr Collins (*straightening his shoulders to an upright posture*) Ah.

Elizabeth What are you doing?

Jane This morning, you challenged me to present you with a suitable suitor.

Elizabeth Mr Collins is no suitor.

Jane Mr Collins, Lizzy, shall I leave the two of you together? Perhaps there is something Mr Collins wishes to tell Lizzy?

Elizabeth Mr Collins must excuse me. He can have nothing to say to me.

Jane Lizzy, I insist upon your staying and hearing Mr Collins.

Jane returns to the writing desk, takes up her pen, and writes rapidly as the scene between Elizabeth and Mr Collins proceeds. Mr Collins now plays his role with chilly dignity

Mr Collins Miss Elizabeth, you can hardly doubt my purpose in approaching you. I think it a right thing for a clergyman to take a wife, and I believe that you are of an age when a woman seeks a husband.

Elizabeth Jane, put down your pen. You are not yourself.

Jane This is the self that I now intend to be. Proceed, Mr Collins.

Mr Collins The establishment that I can offer you is desirable, and I am prepared to perform the offices of a husband conscientiously.

Elizabeth Jane, what are you doing?

Mr Collins Therefore, I respectfully request your hand in marriage.

Jane (*writing*) "Elizabeth weighed Mr Collins' words carefully and made her decision —— "

Elizabeth — to refuse him as courteously as possible.

Jane No.

Elizabeth You cannot mean for me to accept Mr Collins.

Jane You cannot intend to resist such a sensible course.

Elizabeth I cannot marry Mr Collins.

Jane You might show some gratitude, Lizzy. I have refashioned him, and have sacrificed a good deal of comedy to provide you with a thoroughly unobjectionable husband.

Elizabeth Think of my sister. She wants me at home to be her confidante. That is my role in your novel, as we agreed.

Jane Upon further reflection, I do not think that you are a proper sort of confidante for my Jane Bennet. She would be better off keeping Miss Elizabeth at a safe distance. My novel can proceed perfectly well without you.

Elizabeth With me, your novel could be something. You said so yourself.

Jane You cause too much trouble, Lizzy.

Elizabeth I do not love Mr Collins.

Jane (*writing*) "And so Elizabeth —— "

Elizabeth This is not sound. You know it is not sound. Would you ever act in this way yourself?

Jane I can only hope that some day, I will have the opportunity to accept a man as settled in life as Mr Collins. You must show me how it is done. "And so Elizabeth and Mr Collins —— "

Elizabeth Jane, if you compel this match, what confidence can ever subsist between us again?

Jane hesitates

Mr Collins My hand is not unworthy of my cousin's acceptance. And, in view of her circumstances, not to mention a certain something about her nature, it is by no means certain that she will ever receive another offer of marriage.

Jane "And so Elizabeth and Mr Collins were married. The bells rang and everybody smiled." Well, Mr Collins, are you ready to escort your wife to her new home?

Mr Collins We must be on our way, my dear. I have a sermon to prepare.

Elizabeth I believe that domestic economy is to be the subject.

Jane Congratulations, Lizzy. What a successful day this has been for you.

Elizabeth I look forward to congratulating you, Miss Austen, when you attain similar success.

Mr Collins offers his arm to Elizabeth

Black-out

ACT II

The drawing room at the home of the Bigg-Withers. Evening, December, 1802.

A card table is positioned C, *surrounded by four chairs. Two chairs and a side table are positioned* UL, *next to a window. The side table is set with four glasses and a decanter containing Madeira wine.* DR *is an outdoor space, currently in darkness. It is set with a garden table and a green shrub*

Jane sits by the side table and works at her needlework, her workbasket at her feet. She wears her hair pinned up. She takes a pair of scissors from her workbasket, cuts a thread, and places the scissors on the table. She occasionally gazes out of the window

Alethea, Cassandra and Harris sit at the card table, each holding a hand of cards

Alethea I bid two chips for your queen of spades.
Cassandra Very well.
Alethea You accept, Cassandra?
Cassandra Yes, Alethea.
Alethea For two chips? Harris, it is impossible to play speculation with the Austen sisters. Cassandra lacks the avarice to drive a proper bargain, and Jane always refuses to play.
Harris (*turning over a card from his hand*) Ace of hearts.
Cassandra (*turning over a card from her hand*) Eight of diamonds.
Alethea (*turning over a card from her hand*) Ace of spades.
Cassandra The game is yours.
Harris My sister always wins.
Alethea I was lucky.
Cassandra It is my sister and I who are lucky to be with such friends at Christmas time.
Alethea Shall we play again? Jane, will you join us?

Pause

Cassandra Jane!

Jane My apologies. I was looking at the moon. There is a full moon tonight. (*She proceeds to the card table and sits in the empty chair*)

Alethea (*Dealing the cards*) Tomorrow we must go sleighing after dinner.

Cassandra We have not been sleighing since we left Hampshire.

Alethea Something must be done to restore the colour to your cheeks.

Cassandra I cannot think of a better remedy than a sleigh ride.

Alethea Neither of you look entirely well. The air in Bath cannot agree with you, and I have never had much faith in the water. You are both creatures of Hampshire. And Hampshire is not the same without you.

Harris I never thought it right for anyone but your father to be our parson.

Alethea Are you happy in Bath?

Cassandra We are settled there now.

Alethea But are you happy?

Cassandra What a question.

Alethea Are you?

Cassandra In a city, there is always something to occupy one's time.

Jane Sometimes one must go out and visit, and sometimes one must stay home and be visited.

Cassandra Of course, we miss the countryside. Your invitation to spend Christmas here was so very welcome. And who but you, Alethea, would have offered to send a carriage for us?

Alethea How else were you to make the journey?

Jane We might have walked.

Cassandra (*embarrassed*) Jane!

Jane What a spectacle we would have made at your threshold, our petticoats splattered with mud.

Alethea The ideas that pop into Jane's head.

Cassandra Jane is joking, of course.

Jane Of course I am. Pay me no mind.

Alethea Well, now that you are here, we shall have Christmas like in the old days, with sleighing and visits to friends and —

Harris —and one of Jane's theatricals in the parlour!

Jane What is the trump suit, Cassandra?

Cassandra (*turning over the top card on the deck*) Hearts.

Alethea Harris's lucky suit.

Harris Be quiet, Alethea.

Alethea If we put on a play, will you be my pageboy as before, Harris?

Harris Jane must write the part for me, with not too many speeches to learn.

Alethea Come hither, page. I have an errand for you. A dispute between the butcher and the miller requires my most urgent intervention. First, take this bottle of distilled newt and bring it to ––

Jane Stop, please.

Alethea You were always rallying us to perform your plays.

Jane That was so long ago.

Harris Then it is time you wrote us a new one.

Jane I cannot write a sketch. I do not write at all any more.

Alethea That must be a weight off your mother's mind. How she would complain to Mamma: "Whenever there is work to be done, Jane hides herself away with a notebook."

Cassandra My sister has not quite lost the habit of hiding herself away.

Jane But no longer with a notebook.

Harris Will anyone bid for my ten of hearts?

Cassandra I pass.

Alethea Jane, you cannot leave my brother's hearts on the table!

Harris (*protesting*) Alethea!

Jane I will not bid this turn.

Alethea I have had enough of cards. Cassandra, did I tell you that I have completed a new design for a table?

Cassandra Have you?

Alethea I must show it to you. My vanity craves your admiration.

Cassandra Very well.

Alethea Harris will not mind keeping Jane amused while we older sisters occupy ourselves as older sisters do.

Jane I was about to retire. It is nearly midnight.

Alethea Nonsense. I know what late hours you city dwellers keep. Harris will entertain you while we matrons confer.

Harris Perhaps we had all better go to bed.

Alethea Not now, Harris. Cassandra will not rest until she has put me to shame with a dozen improvements to my design. And I am sure that Jane is determined to conquer all the hearts in the deck.

Jane But Harris is tired ––

Alethea If we quit you now, you will think us very dull hosts. (*She draws Cassandra to one side*)

Jane We had best continue playing for Alethea's sake. (*She draws a card from the deck and turns it over*) Three of hearts.

Harris I bid one chip for it.

Jane For a three?

Harris Two chips, then.

Jane For such a low card?

Harris I mean, I do not bid at all — Or else, I bid all my chips, to have done with the game — I mean — I hardly know what I mean.

Jane Shall we set the cards aside?
Harris Not if it amuses you to play.
Jane I am always amused in this house.
Harris You have been happy here?
Jane Our friends are endlessly kind to us.
Harris You have been our friend for a long time.
Jane With my twenty-seventh birthday a fortnight away, I have been doing most things for a long time.
Harris You have lived in Bath for a long time.
Jane It certainly feels that way.
Harris Alethea said that your parents moved to Bath so that you and Cassandra would find husbands.
Jane If that was their hope, the experiment has provided little in the way of satisfaction.
Harris "Why should Miss Austen go to Bath to find a husband?" I said to Alethea.
Jane And for that matter, why should Miss Austen find a husband in Bath? It is late. (*She stands up*) We really ought to set the cards aside.
Harris (*standing up*) You are angry with me. I have said the wrong thing.
Jane Of course not.
Harris That is a habit with me — saying the wrong thing. Other men come ready with all the right words. And all the right gestures. Like that tall fellow, Lefroy. (*Mimicking Tom*) "I know how difficult it is to tear one's self away from a fine pair of eyes in the face of a pretty woman. And so, to assist you, I volunteer to escort Miss Austen in the next set." (*He tries to whirl Jane around, but stumbles*) Oh bother!
Jane Never mind, Harris. Mr Lefroy hardly proved to be a formidable rival in the end. Though the papers say that he is a fierce adversary in the courtroom.
Harris He is now married.
Jane Is he? Of course he is. Why shouldn't he be? (*Pause*) We are not so different, you and I. I never seem to behave quite as I should, myself.
Harris Exactly! That is what I always said. That is why I said that we should marry.
Jane Because Miss Jane Austen is very ill-behaved?
Harris I said it on the night of our ball.
Jane You are fortunate that gentlemen of twenty-one are not held to all the declarations they made at fifteen.
Harris You and I are exactly alike.
Jane Are we?

Harris You just said so yourself. Making people laugh when we don't mean to be funny.

Jane For what do we live but to make sport for our neighbours?

Harris If we were married, we should not care if they laughed. We should not care what other people thought.

Jane How Alethea would scold you for teasing a spinster like this.

Harris You would not be a spinster if we were married. And we would all be so comfortable by the fire.

Jane With you in your slippers.

Harris You remember about my slippers!

Jane Of course, I do. Dear boy, you were so earnest.

Harris And I'll warrant that you even remember where I keep them.

Jane Under your bed.

Harris You do remember! You remember because you care for me. You do! I knew it!

Alethea What is it, Harris? Have you something to tell us?

Harris (*alarmed*) Nothing, Alethea.

Alethea I am such a fool. Ignore me. Pretend I am not in the room.

Jane Of course I care for you. You are Alethea's brother.

Harris And you would be her sister if . . . you know . . . if —

Jane Do you really think that I would make you a proper sort of wife?

Harris Is that your worry? If that is your only worry, that is no worry at all. We shall be married. We shall. Alethea! Cassandra! Jane and I are to be married!

Alethea Oh, Jane!

Harris We shall be married in the New Year.

Alethea We have been waiting for so long to wish you joy.

Jane Then . . . you must wait no longer.

Alethea What a wonderful Christmas we will have!

Cassandra Congratulations, Jane.

Alethea You have made us all so happy. How I laughed to see Harris stumble and blush all evening, as if he half expected Jane to turn him down, poor lamb.

Harris It was only that I did not know how to begin. Then suddenly we were in the middle of it all, and a moment later everything was settled.

Alethea We shall be just as dear to one another as if we had been born sisters. We must celebrate! Harris, come help me fetch the Madeira.

Alethea and Harris fetch the decanter and glasses from the side table

Jane Cassandra, you will come live with us, of course.

Cassandra Steady! It is a bit early to begin filling your husband's house with lodgers!

Jane You will have a carriage and a horse, and you will take air every day. And you will have a chair of your own by the fire, where you are to sit and do absolutely nothing at least once a day. Please tell me that you are happy.

Cassandra We must send word to Mamma.

Jane Do you think that she will finally leave off fretting about what is to become of us?

Alethea and Harris fill the glasses with Madeira

Elizabeth enters

Alethea To Jane and Harris.

Cassandra To Jane and Harris.

Harris offers a glass to Jane. Elizabeth intercepts, and snatches the glass away

Elizabeth To Jane and Harris. May the bride look as happy on her wedding day as she does tonight. (*She drains the glass and hands it back to Jane*)

Jane Lizzy? What are you doing here?

Elizabeth Fine words of welcome!

Harris We must marry in January!

Jane So soon?

Alethea I detest long engagements.

Harris We shall announce it at our Christmas party, right after Jane's theatrical.

Jane I told you, I cannot write a theatrical.

Elizabeth Shall we ask Miss Austen the reason for this?

Jane I no longer write.

Elizabeth Shall we ask Miss Austen why she no longer writes?

Jane Because ... I suppose, because there is nothing to write about.

Elizabeth No suitable subject presents itself to a woman of intelligence and experience?

Jane Bath is too full of business and bustle to allow for writing.

Elizabeth And no woman has ever turned her back on the business and bustle of the world to spend half an hour at her writing desk?

Jane What does it matter to you whether I write or not?

Elizabeth The evenings are long at this time of year. A woman often wishes for a volume of sense and wit penned by one of her own sex. Or, if none is to be had, a few pages of folly and nonsense would do.

Jane I tried to publish Jane Bennet's story, but it came to nothing. Mr Cadell's reply came quickly enough. "Declined by return of post".

Elizabeth And there are no other publishers in England?

Alethea You sent a novel to a publisher, Jane?

Jane I am sorry, Alethea. I hardly realized that I was speaking out loud.

Alethea You have since abandoned such ideas?

Cassandra Jane meant to publish anonymously, of course.

Alethea Even so. Word always gets out.

Jane You must be pleased with yourself, Elizabeth Bennet. Barely do you make an entrance, and all is confusion. Even after all these years.

Elizabeth Elizabeth Bennet? Must I remind you that I have been Elizabeth Collins for nearly seven years? (*She reaches into the workbasket and retrieves a small notebook, which she hands to Jane*) For the particulars concerning my nuptials, consult page forty-two of your manuscript—declined by return of post.

Alethea What would you think, Harris, if your sister were to set about publishing novels?

Harris Do you write novels, Alethea?

Alethea With a home to look after, and a brother to care for? I should think not. We must send to London for the wedding cake.

Cassandra I am sure that between us, Mamma and I can contrive to bake a cake.

Alethea We will order it first thing in the morning.

Harris And I will ride to town directly after breakfast.

Alethea How like a man to escape at the first mention of wedding plans. What do you think of this brother of mine, Jane, dashing off and leaving his bride behind?

Harris (*to Jane*) I will ride into town to set a lock of your hair into a ring.

Jane What a notion.

Harris That is what people do when they become engaged. Setting locks of hair into rings and that sort of thing.

Alethea Harris! I never knew you were a romantic.

Harris You must give me a lock of your hair.

Jane Of course ... Of course.

Harris Straight away. The scissors —

Harris proceeds to the side table. As he reaches for the scissors, Elizabeth confiscates them

Elizabeth Pardon. This pair belongs to me.

Jane They came from my workbasket.

Elizabeth I once loaned them to you at a ball. Have you forgotten?

Jane How very like you to choose this moment to remind me.
Harris I was sure there was a pair of scissors on the table.
Jane We can look for them in the morning. My hair is pinned up.
Harris The scissors must be in your workbasket.

Harris rummages in the workbasket for the scissors

Jane Lizzy, the scissors!
Elizabeth I am going out to cut some Christmas greens to bring back to the parsonage. Mr Collins is very fond of greenery.
Jane (*to Harris*) Perhaps I left the scissors in the garden when I was gathering Christmas greens.
Elizabeth Good-night! (*She proceeds to the outdoor space*)
Jane Lizzy!

Holding the manuscript, Jane follows Elizabeth. The lights crossfade to reveal the garden table and green shrub. Jane may tuck the manuscript into her costume, or set it down on the garden table

Alethea, Cassandra and Harris exit

Give me back the scissors, Lizzy. My future husband has requested a lock of my hair and he must have one.

Elizabeth snips a few pieces of greenery with the scissors

Stop teasing. I must return to my friends, and I mean to return with the scissors.
Elizabeth Find another pair.
Jane You are jealous.
Elizabeth Who would not envy you? Only think of the fine clothes and fine carriages you will have. You, who once aspired merely to a husband as settled in life as Mr Collins.
Jane My good fortune comes at a high price.
Elizabeth Does it?
Jane Did I not give you up?
Elizabeth Judging by how pleased you are to see me, my absence has been no sacrifice.
Jane No sacrifice? My novel was to ring with your laughter and instead, I was left with the murmurs of a dutiful Jane Bennet. And if my novel suffered for want of laughter, I have suffered still more. Lizzy, I have been so lonely.
Elizabeth No longer, my dear. You shall have a husband.

Jane Why do you insist on taunting me?

Elizabeth I am off. Your friends are waiting for you and I must be on my way.

Jane Do not leave me, Lizzy.

Elizabeth I must get back to the parsonage to prepare the chickens' feed. I have lately discovered that adding a little milk to their mash has a most salutary effect on their plumage.

Jane Promise me that you will come back. Promise me that you will come back every day.

Elizabeth Is that all?

Jane Or rather, every night. Just as you once said. After Mrs Harris Bigg-Wither sends her husband to bed, she will creep downstairs, candle in hand, to unlock her writing desk and confer with you. Oh, Lizzy! What novels we will write.

Elizabeth What need will Mrs Harris Bigg-Wither have for invention? Her own home will furnish everything she desires.

Jane How could I ever have thought that when I married, I would not need to write? It is married women who must write. If married women are to behave as they must, they must have some reprieve. (*Pause*) Lizzy, you will be more than my reprieve. You will be my reward. I had to send you away because you were too dangerous a companion for a single woman. But now that I am to be married, you are no longer a threat.

Elizabeth Is that meant to be a compliment?

Jane If you are no longer a danger, I can write about you again. And that is why I must marry. So that, once again, I will be free to write about my very own unruly, impertinent Lizzy. What fun we will have!

Elizabeth Jane, you forget something. For the past seven years, unruly, impertinent Lizzy has been good Mrs Collins, the parson's wife.

Jane What can seven years mean to a character in a novel?

Elizabeth Seven years of marriage can mean a great deal. I have worked hard to fulfil my new role. In consequence, you may find me a rather dull subject for your pen.

Jane You?

Elizabeth Will you document my little discovery about the salutary effect of adding milk to the chickens' mash? Will you record that every Saturday, my husband dictates a lengthy sermon which I take down in a meticulous hand, and that on Sunday, I listen attentively to his delivery as I sit in my pew with folded hands and downcast eyes? Or will you describe the visits bestowed upon me by my esteemed patroness, Lady Catherine de Bourgh?

Lady Catherine enters. Elizabeth's manner toward her is demure and restrained

Elizabeth Good-evening, Lady Catherine.

Lady Catherine I have come from the parsonage, Mrs Collins.

Elizabeth Your Ladyship is too kind in her attentions to us.

Lady Catherine I had expected to find you there.

Elizabeth Allow me to apologize, Lady Catherine. I have been calling on an old acquaintance. Of course, I would have postponed my trip instantly, had I known that you were to favour us with a visit.

Lady Catherine Your maid informed me that you were out visiting. She also informed me that you travelled unaccompanied.

Elizabeth Miss Austen has just received an offer of marriage. I came to congratulate her on her engagement.

Lady Catherine I presume that once again, Miss Austen, you have failed to inform your parents of your plans.

Elizabeth I can assure Your Ladyship that this is an entirely different sort of match. This time, there can be no objection from any quarter. Our visit draws to a close, and I am about to return home.

Lady Catherine Again, unaccompanied?

Elizabeth I mean no offence, Your Ladyship.

Jane Lizzy, why do you demean yourself like this? How can you tolerate her?

Elizabeth (*to Jane*) You must realize that the Collins' fortunes depend entirely upon Lady Catherine's favour.

Lady Catherine I will send for a servant to see you home.

Elizabeth I should hate to put you to such trouble, Lady Catherine. Perhaps someone else could be found —

Mr Darcy enters

—to escort me.

Mr Darcy If you would allow me, Mrs Collins, I should be most happy to assist.

Lady Catherine Fitzwilliam!

Mr Darcy The parsonage lies on my intended route.

Jane What is Mr Darcy doing here?

Elizabeth (*to Jane*) Oh, I neglected to tell you. It is a habit with Mr Darcy to call at the parsonage when he visits his aunt.

Jane How odd that he should visit the marriage home of the woman who rejected his proposal.

Elizabeth At first, I supposed that his object was to make me feel what I had lost in refusing him. But I have since changed my view.

Jane What a trial his visits must be for you.

Elizabeth Mr Darcy rather improves upon acquaintance.

Jane I suppose he visits Lady Catherine to pay his respects to her daughter, the very eligible Miss de Bourgh.

Elizabeth Lady Catherine certainly seems to think so.

Lady Catherine Mrs Collins, I stopped by the parsonage to inform you that we can dispense with your company tomorrow evening. My nephew has surprised us with a visit, and my daughter and I will be greatly occupied in consequence.

Mr Darcy Please do not cancel the Collins' invitation on my account, Aunt.

Lady Catherine I am sure that you and my daughter will wish to converse on subjects best suited to an intimate family gathering. Speaking of family, Mrs Collins, do you continue to take Mr Nelson's snail water?

Elizabeth Yes, Lady Catherine.

Lady Catherine Every evening?

Elizabeth Directly before retiring to bed.

Lady Catherine It is essential that the preparation be taken last thing at night. I always insist on that point.

Elizabeth I thank you for your concern.

Lady Catherine The parsonage must have children, and the more the better. There is no greater proponent of large families than me. My daughter and I are both fervent spokeswomen on this point. (*Pause*) Is it true, Miss Austen, that you have accepted a proposal of marriage?

Jane Yes I have, Your Ladyship.

Lady Catherine I will instruct Mr Nelson to send you a bottle of snail water directly.

Jane Thank you, Lady Catherine.

Lady Catherine Fitzwilliam, I will expect you for supper tomorrow. We keep a most punctual table.

Mr Darcy So you have reminded me, Aunt Catherine. Three times.

Lady Catherine exits

Elizabeth I am indebted to you, Mr Darcy, for delivering me from the good offices of your aunt.

Mr Darcy My Aunt Catherine means well, but I must apologize for her mode of expression.

Elizabeth Lady Catherine does love to be of use.

Mr Darcy Her assistance has been invaluable as it has procured me your company for an hour.

Elizabeth Or even two, depending on our route.

Mr Darcy The path over the hillock offers a stirring view of the moon.

Elizabeth How long will you remain in the neighbourhood this time, Mr Darcy?

Mr Darcy My aunt will not countenance a visit of less than a month.

Elizabeth Neither would Mr Collins. Or his wife.

Jane Elizabeth? Mr Darcy? This is most peculiar.

Elizabeth Peculiar friendships are the offspring of peculiar marriages, Jane.

Jane This cannot be! I know it to be impossible. He is the man who tried to separate your sister from Mr Bingley.

Mr Darcy I have since conceded that I was in error on that point.

Elizabeth You transcribed his apology yourself, on page two hundred and seven. Though you failed to do justice to the depth of his feelings.

Jane Do you love him, Lizzy?

Elizabeth My marriage would be unendurable, but for his visits. And occasionally, in his company, I feel myself to be something of the woman I once was. (*Teasingly*) How very trying for you, Mr Darcy, that you should bring out in me the very qualities that rendered me so unfit to be the wife of the man who governs Pemberley.

Mr Darcy Do not remind me of my words on that day. You can scarcely conceive how they have tortured me. If I had known then how to value your spirit as I do now, if my proposal had acknowledged more of your worth, and less of my pride, perhaps I would have spoken to better effect. My suit might have found a more willing ear, and even now, the halls of Pemberley might be ringing with the laughter of its rightful mistress.

Pause

Jane What a woman could you have been, Lizzy, had I allowed you such a marriage?

Elizabeth No more, both of you.

Jane What have I done to you? What have I done in marrying you to Mr Collins?

Elizabeth There is little use in brooding over it now.

Jane Could your marriage not be . . . ended?

Elizabeth A likely turn of events.

Jane Do you never dream that some chance occurrence might set you free?

Elizabeth What do you think?

Lady Catherine enters

Lady Catherine Think? It is unthinkable! How dare you talk of such matters? Impudent girls!

In the course of the ensuing exchange, Elizabeth gradually regains her former assertiveness

Elizabeth Lady Catherine!

Mr Darcy Aunt Catherine, were you spying on us?

Lady Catherine I am shocked and astonished at what I have overheard, Mrs Collins. Do you, Mrs Elizabeth Collins, actually dare to imagine yourself married to my nephew, my own nephew, Mr Darcy? Is this your gratitude for my attentions to you?

Elizabeth I was only ——

Lady Catherine You must know that Mr Darcy is engaged to my daughter.

Mr Darcy Engaged? Aunt Catherine, what do you mean?

Lady Catherine You have always been intended for one another. Your mother and I planned your union while you were in your cradles.

Mr Darcy You cannot bring about a marriage by planning it, Aunt Catherine.

Lady Catherine Fitzwilliam, this woman's allurements have made you forget your duty. She must relinquish her hold upon you at once. Promise me, Mrs Collins, that you will never consort with my nephew again.

Pause

Elizabeth I will make no promise of the kind.

Lady Catherine Obstinate, headstrong girl! I shall not go away till you have given me the assurance I require.

Elizabeth And I certainly never shall give it.

Lady Catherine Allow me to remind you that the livelihood of your family is at my command.

Elizabeth Your Ladyship wants Mr Darcy to marry your daughter, but would my giving you the promise you demand make their marriage more probable? Would my refusing to speak to Mr Darcy prompt him to propose to his cousin?

Lady Catherine I had hoped that your marriage would cure you of your youthful insolence. Miss Austen, you must compel Mrs Collins to do as I bid.

Jane I am done with compelling Lizzy to do anything.

Lady Catherine Then beware the consequences. And not only for her, but for yourself. If Mrs Collins unites herself with Mr Darcy, will you be satisfied with Mr Bigg-Wither? How will you bring yourself to proceed with your marriage?

Harris (*off stage*) Jane!

Jane Worse yet, if I proceed with my marriage, how will I bring myself to write about Elizabeth Bennet and Mr Darcy?
Harris (*off stage*) Jane!
Jane The contrast with my own situation would be intolerable.

Harris enters

Harris Here you are! Have you been outside for all this time?
Jane I lost track of the time.
Harris Doing what?
Jane Oh ... admiring the garden in the moonlight. It is a lovely garden.

Harris tries to kiss Jane. She moves away

Harris You left us to fetch the scissors, so that I might cut a lock of your hair.
Jane I was just collecting my thoughts.
Harris Well? Did you find them?
Jane My thoughts?
Harris The scissors.
Jane I was about to —
Harris Never mind. I have my penknife with me. It will do.
Jane Harris, I do not think —
Harris Just a small lock —

Harris advances with the knife

Jane No!

Elizabeth intercedes between Jane and Harris, brandishing the scissors to fend him off, as Jane manoeuvres herself out of Harris's reach

Elizabeth Leave her be!
Jane Harris, put your knife down!
Harris I do not understand you.

Jane takes the scissors from Elizabeth, shows them to Harris, shakes her head sadly and tucks the scissors into her sash

Jane I cannot give you a lock of my hair, Harris. I cannot give you a lock of my hair because —
Harris Because your hair is pinned up.
Jane No, because —

Harris Because it is all so sudden?

Jane It is because ——

Harris I was only asking for what you gave so easily to another.

Jane Harris, I cannot give you a lock of my hair because I cannot marry you.

Lady Catherine So this is your final resolve. I am most seriously displeased.

Lady Catherine exits

Harris You said that we were to be married. Alethea and Cassandra were in the room, and we all drank Madeira to celebrate.

Jane My behaviour has been abominable.

Harris You are unwell.

Jane I am perfectly well.

Harris You have taken a chill. You are not yourself.

Jane This is the only self that I can be. Please hear me as a rational creature.

Harris Rational? When I offer you everything and you refuse it all?

Jane Dear, dear Harris. If we were to marry, I would come to despise myself, and bring out the worst in you.

Harris Do you not wish for marriage?

Jane So much so that I must refuse your offer.

Harris You are waiting for a better one?

Jane I think it unlikely. Particularly if I insist on hiding myself away with a notebook dreaming up marriages for my heroines.

Harris You said that you no longer write.

Jane I have left my pen idle for far too long.

Harris You will be spinsters all your lives, you and Cassandra both. You will shiver in cramped rooms with your parents, when you might have been mistress of this house. You will be ridiculous.

Harris exits

Jane watches him leave and turns to Elizabeth

Jane What a lot of trouble you cause, Lizzy.

Elizabeth Is that your way of thanking me?

Elizabeth and Jane look at one another and laugh

Jane I must do better than thank you. (*Taking the manuscript*) I must undo your marriage.

Elizabeth Is it possible?

Jane Everything is possible in a novel. We must go back to the manuscript. Mr Collins must be restored to what he was when you first encountered him, and you must refuse him. Now, how to recreate Mr Collins? (*Writing*) "Miss Elizabeth," he said, "I am no opponent of dance"— no, that was not it — "I hope Miss Elizabeth will think me no stranger to respectable balls"—No! How could I have thrown my best work away?

Elizabeth (*retrieving the discarded manuscript fragment from her costume*) I believe that Mr Collins's exact words were, "To the contrary, Miss Elizabeth, I am by no means of the opinion that —— "

Jane The ballroom scene with Mr Collins! You kept it for me all these years! (*She seizes the page and reads from it*) "To the contrary, Miss Elizabeth, I am by no means of the opinion that a ball of this kind, given by an established family can have any evil tendency —— "

Mr Collins enters

Mr Collins — and I am so far from objecting to dancing myself that I shall take this opportunity of soliciting your hand.

Jane Welcome back, Mr Collins.

Mr Collins bows to Jane, who coaches him back into his former manners and posture

I believe that it is not for the dance alone that you wish to solicit the hand of Miss Elizabeth Bennet.

Elizabeth (*joyfully*) Am I to be Miss Elizabeth Bennet again?

Jane You are. The scissors. (*She takes the scissors from her sash and scores out a page from the manuscript*) Your marriage to Mr Collins. (*She tears up the excised page*) Once again, you are the unmarried daughter of a country gentleman.

Elizabeth My papa's education rather exceeds his income.

Jane You are the sworn enemy of proud Mr Darcy, who snubbed you at a dance — though you will admit that a man of his distinction has a right to be proud.

Elizabeth I could easily forgive his pride if he had not mortified mine.

Jane And, what is more, you are about to receive a proposal of marriage.

Elizabeth Am I?

Jane From a most singular gentleman.

Elizabeth Not Mr ——

Jane Is that not so, Mr Collins?

Mr Collins I see no reason for delay. A prompt marriage is the particular recommendation of the very noble lady whom I have the honour of calling patroness. And almost as soon as I was introduced to Miss Bennet, I singled her out as the companion of my future life. (T*urning his attention to Elizabeth*) And now, nothing remains but for me to assure you, Miss Elizabeth, of the violence of my affection, and for you to name the day that will make me the happiest of men.

Elizabeth You are too hasty, sir. I am sensible of the honour of your proposals, but I cannot do otherwise than decline them.

Mr Collins I am not now to learn that it is usual with young ladies to reject the addresses of the man whom they secretly mean to accept and that sometimes the refusal is repeated a second or even a third time.

Elizabeth Sir, I am perfectly serious in my refusal.

Mr Collins You are trying to increase my love by suspense, according to the usual practice of elegant females.

Elizabeth Do not consider me now as an elegant female intending to plague you, but please hear me as a rational creature speaking the truth from her heart.

Mr Collins You are uniformly charming!

Elizabeth Mr Collins, you could not make me happy, and I am the last woman in the world who would make you so. Were your friend Lady Catherine to know me, she would find me wanting in every respect.

Mr Collins Were it certain that Lady Catherine would think so...

Jane I should have warned you, Mr Collins. Lizzy can be a very headstrong, foolish girl.

Mr Collins Oh. If she really is so very headstrong and foolish, I do not know whether she would altogether be a very desirable wife ... Especially when compared to some of the other young ladies in the neighbourhood. Miss Austen must excuse me.

Mr Collins exits purposefully

Jane How quickly men in novels recover their spirits. It will not be so easy for poor Harris.

Mr Darcy A man of sense will ultimately value honest words from a clear-thinking woman.

Jane I do not think that many would judge my conduct tonight as clear-thinking.

Mr Darcy Then you must be your own judge, and temper your verdict with charity.

Jane Thank you, Mr Darcy.

Elizabeth What is he doing here?

Jane Patience, Lizzy. The day will come when you receive his company with joy.

Elizabeth With scorn, I should think.

Jane And not only his company, but his proposal as well.

Elizabeth If there is joy to be had in refusing a proposal.

Jane Yes, I believe you will refuse his proposal. That is, you will refuse his first proposal. But he is as determined as he his proud. And he will prove himself worthy of your hand.

Elizabeth Is he to rescue me from some terrible crisis?

Jane With so many of your sisters at the age of unreason, I am sure I can produce at least one credible calamity to test my hero's mettle.

Elizabeth So proud Mr Darcy replaces charming Mr Bingley as your hero?

Jane What is more, I must warn you that you are in grave danger of replacing pretty Jane Bennet as my heroine.

Elizabeth I told you that I would never do for a heroine. At least do not make me a model heroine.

Jane You will still be permitted to disappear on solitary rambles in the rain, and to splatter your petticoats with mud.

Cassandra enters

Cassandra Jane!

Jane Cassandra, dear Cassandra. Have you heard the news?

Cassandra I was about to climb the stairs when Harris stormed into the drawing room. What he told me, is it true? Did you really break off your engagement?

Jane nods

We cannot stay here any longer. We must ask our friends for their forgiveness, and beg them for their carriage to convey us home.

Jane How will we explain it all to Mamma and Papa?

Cassandra Alethea may never speak to us again.

Jane What will become of us, Cassandra, when we no longer have Papa's income to sustain us?

Cassandra You must not think of that.

Jane But you and Mamma do.

Cassandra Jane, I have never felt so . . . so . . . Oh! (*Her mood changes abruptly to jubilation*) You refused him! You refused him! Thank God you refused him!

Jane But this house was to be our home. This garden was to be ours.

Cassandra Jane, if you were determined to be mistress of all of this, how could I ever advise you to do otherwise? But I would have you do anything rather than marry without affection.

Jane Cassandra, I had no idea!

Elizabeth I suppose that I should thank you, Mr Darcy, for your kind words to Miss Austen. There are moments in a woman's life when she urgently requires the support of her friends, and therefore, let me thank you in her name.

Mr Darcy If you will thank me, let it be for yourself alone. In speaking, I thought only of you.

Elizabeth Why, Mr Darcy!

Jane Cassandra?

Cassandra Yes?

Jane Do you remember my failed novel about Jane Bennet and Mr Bingley?

Cassandra Your novel was not a failure. It was only —

Jane – promptly rejected by Mr. Cadell. Do you remember Jane's sister, Elizabeth?

Cassandra The one who married the tiresome clergyman?

Jane Suppose that I were to revise my novel. Suppose that instead of marrying Mr Collins, Elizabeth is pursued by Mr Bingley's friend, Mr Darcy.

Cassandra That tall gentleman with the estate in Derbyshire?

Jane nods

Mr Darcy is such a brooding, unpleasant sort of man. But what of it, if Elizabeth really liked him?

Jane Perhaps Mr Darcy is not quite so unpleasant as we thought. Or at least, perhaps he is capable of reform. And how he speaks. Listen.

Jane indicates Elizabeth and Mr Darcy. For the first time, Cassandra is able to see and hear the fictional characters

Mr Darcy Miss Bennet, I have been a selfish creature all my life. As a child, I was given good principles, but left to follow them in pride and conceit. You have shown me how insufficient all my pretensions were to please a woman worthy of being pleased. By you, I have been properly humbled. You are too generous to trifle with me. If your feelings are still what they were when I last proposed, tell me so at once. My affections and wishes remain unchanged, but one word from you will silence me on this subject forever.

Music begins to play

Elizabeth Do you not feel a great inclination, Mr Darcy, to seize this opportunity to dance a reel?

Mr Darcy Dearest, loveliest Elizabeth.

Mr Darcy offers Elizabeth his hand. They begin to dance and then embrace

Jane You see, Mr Darcy will ——

Cassandra You may tell me all about it when we are on our way.

Jane We must pack our trunks.

Cassandra You know, Jane, Mr Cadell is not the only publisher in England.

Jane Indeed.

Cassandra Perhaps one could yet be found who would look with favour on your Elizabeth Bennet and her Mr Darcy.

Jane Can there be anything more ridiculous than an ageing spinster publishing novels that teach the admiring multitude what love really is? Jane Austen will be ridiculous. Jane Austen will be utterly ridiculous. Jane Austen will be utterly, absurdly, laughably, unashamedly, joyfully, ridiculously ridiculous.

Cassandra Jane Austen will be an author.

CURTAIN

FURNITURE AND PROPERTY LIST

ACT 1

Scene 1

On stage: Games table
Around it: Three chairs

Personal: **Mr Darcy/Tom**: hand of cards
Mr Bingley/Harris/Mr Collins: hand of cards
Madame Lefroy: hand of cards
Jane: shawl, handkerchief, reticule containing notebook and small pencil, lock of hair
Elizabeth: small pair of scissors (tucked into her sash)

Scene 2

Set: Writing desk. *On it:* pens, inkwell, paper and notebook (Jane's manuscript)
Three chairs
Pile of garments for mending
Workbasket. *In it*: scissors, needle and thread

Off stage: Hat and gloves (**Mr Darcy**)
Letter (**Mrs Austen)**
Lock of hair tied with piece of ribbon from Scene 1 (**Tom**)

ACT 2

Set: Card table. *On it*: piles of chips and deck of cards. *Around it*: four chairs
Decanter. *In it*: Madeira
Four glasses
Side table and two chairs
Garden table
Greenery

Re-set: Workbasket. *In it*: scissors, notebook (Jane's manuscript)

Personal: **Jane**: needle and thread and a piece of needlework
Alethea: hand of cards
Cassandra: hand of cards
Harris: hand of cards, penknife
Elizabeth: manuscript fragment (from Scene 2)

LIGHTING PLOT

ACT 1

Scene 1

To open: *Evening interior lighting*

Cue 1: **Madame Lefroy** and **Elizabeth** exit (Page 16)
Black-out, or if stage is already set for Scene 2, lights crossfade to the Austens' parlour, UR

Scene 2

To open: *Daytime interior lighting*

Cue 1: **Mr Collins** offers his arm to **Elizabeth** (Page 33)
Black-out

ACT 2

To open: *Evening interior lighting*

Cue 1: **Jane:** "Lizzy!" (Page 41)
Lights crossfade to garden (lights to imitate moonlight)

EFFECTS PLOT

ACT 1
Scene 1

To open: *Regency period dance music plays and then fades gradually*

Cue 1: **Mr Bingley**: "...to form your acquaintance" (Page 3)
Music begins

Cue 2: **Mr Darcy**: "...such tiresome company" (Page 3)
Music ends abruptly

Cue 3: **Jane** jots down a note in her notebook (Page 7)
Music begins

Cue 4: **Harris:** "...always know where to find them." (Page 8)
Music ends

Cue 5: **Mr Collins**: "Delightful!" (Page 13)
Music begins again

Cue 6: **Jane** presents the lock of hair to Tom (Page 14)
Music ends

Cue 7: **Mr Darcy** looks at **Elizabeth**, looks away and looks at her again (Page 15)
Reel music begins

Cue 8: **Mr Darcy** exits (Page 15)
Music fades

Scene 2

Cue 1: **Jane**: "...what is there for her to do, but sew? (Page 25)
The doorbell rings

ACT 2

Cue 1: **Mr Darcy**: "... silence me on this subject forever." (Page 52)
Music begins to play